**W9-DDD-886**

Sketching the Concept

# Sketching the Concept
## Perspective Illustration for Architects, Designers and Artists

Harold Linton and Scott Sutton

DESIGN PRESS

Dedicated to Nancy and Robert L. Sutton

First Edition, Second Printing
Copyright © 1993 by Harold Linton and Scott Sutton
Printed in Hong Kong by Everbest Printing Co.

Library of Congress Cataloging-in-Publication Data

Linton, Harold.
    Sketching the concept / Harold Linton and Scott Sutton.—1st ed.
       p.   cm.
    Includes bibliographical references and index.
    ISBN 0-8306-4070-3
    1. Architectural drawing.    2. Architectural design.    I. Sutton,
Scott.   II. Title.
NA2700.L547   1992
720′.28′4—dc20                        91–38185
                                       CIP

Design Press
11 West 19th Street
New York, NY 10011

Design Press books are published by Design Press, an imprint of TAB BOOKS. TAB BOOKS is a Division of McGraw-Hill, Inc. The Design Press logo is a trademark of TAB BOOKS.

Page 2
Vignette composition with building in the distance. Pen-and-ink. United Technologies's Pratt & Whitney jet engine rebuild facility. Southington, Connecticut. Giffels Associates, Inc.

page 6
Street study of Ann Arbor, Michigan. Felt pen on paper. Designer unknown.

page 8
High-rise office complex. Pen-and-ink with wash. Designer unknown.

page 10
Study drawing for the residence of James Blain, Architect. Pen-and-ink.

# Contents

# Acknowledgments

Richard Rochon years ago opened my eyes to the many wonders of fine architectural drawing and painting, particularly the works of Robert L. Sutton; I am indebted to him for many ideas incorporated in these pages. Professor Don Kersten, professor of art at the University of Michigan, organized the first retrospective exhibition of Bob's work at the University of Michigan in 1990 and kindly shared many of his insights with me. Al Blair, Harry Vaporciyan, Harold Van Dine, Jim Blain, Paul Butala, Robert B. Alpern, Bill Ku, Dave Sellards, and Elmore Leonard all worked closely with Bob and generously loaned drawings and shared background information with me. The following offices and friends supported the University of Michigan exhibition of Bob's work in 1990 and, in turn, gave momentum and support to this project: Harley Ellington Pierce Yee and Associates; Yamasaki and Associates; Giffels Associates, Architects; BEI Associates, Inc.; Redstone Architects; Rossetti Associates Architects; Architectural Images; Solomon, Cordwell, Buenz and Associates, Inc.; Pei Cobb Freed & Partners; David H. Lawrence; Bruce Boore; Dan Kaplan; Dick Yocum; Nicholas Pastor; Fred Mayer; All Hutt; Carl Luckenback; Bill Martin; Bob Rogers; Bill Wizinsky; Sam Dorchen; The Maunders Company, Inc.; Harold Binder; Cornell F. Mays; Louis and Grace Jelsch; Ruth Coulson; Alex Weston; Michael and Shirley Glass; Bill Felsenfeld; Mr. and Mrs. Douglas M. Parrish; Gordon McGowan; and Charles Shridde.

I wish to thank Dr. Richard Marburger, Dr. Robert Ellis, and Dr. Neville H. Clouten of Lawrence Technological University for their inspired views about the study of architectural illustration and support; Harvey Ferrero and Gretchen Maricak for providing background materials and for innumerable suggestions on drawing; my colleagues in the College of Architecture and Design at Lawrence Technological University—William Allen, Roy J. Strickfaden, Tom Regenbogen, Steve Rost, Tom Nashlen, Richard Hall, Garnet Cousins, Dan Price, John Sheoris, Gretchen Maricak, Harvey Ferrero, Robert Carr, David Miller, Ken Miller, Betty-Lee Seydler-Sweatt, and Nancy McCurdy—who consistently offer support and advice while challenging our students to excel in graphic and design education.

Every attempt has been made to locate the original designers of illustrated projects in this book. A few could not be found. We would be pleased to know who they might be, to credit them in a future edition.

I also wish to thank those institutions that have loaned work and given their permission to reproduce significant artwork for this project, including the Museum of Modern Art, New York; The Art Institute of Chicago; and The Architectural League of New York. I am indebted to my friend and assistant, Laura Fritzler; my colleague Gretchen Rudy for her interest, advice, and encouragement in bringing this project to publication; and to Wally Bizon for photographic assistance. And finally, to my wife, Nadyne Linton, and Scott's wife, Patricia Burns Sutton, for their devotion, patience, perseverance, and love during the creation of this book.

HAROLD LINTON

# Foreword

Drawing, in its various forms and media, plays an integral role in the architectural design process. Much has been written about this process by well-known contemporary and historical members of the design professions, addressing the many avenues of communication: the generative sketch, with which design concepts are conceived and communicated; the preparation of initial study sketches and drawings, which act to refine and unify an idea during its evolution; and finally the representative drawing, which attempts to communicate the design intention to others accurately.

In the discussion of sketching for the architectural design process that follows, the focus is on the illustrator. The essence of sketching the concept is capturing pictorial ideas as they occur to the illustrator in early phases of design study. The special skills of the illustrator are most apparent in the visualization of a building that exists only as schematic and plan drawings. Combined with the illustrator's own imagination and analysis, the initial dialogs, graphic studies, and models form a basis for a translation of the design concept into the earliest visual metaphors. In conversations with the project manager in the architectural office, the illustrator probes for information that will unlock his or her own creative initiative. This unique relationship between the illustrator and the project manager or design team involves both specific and general communication.

During conversations with the project manager, the illustrator becomes attuned to the most significant attributes of the design concept. Making mental notes of visual information, using one's mind almost like a camera to make snapshots of specific details as well as broader, more expansive information, he or she distills the essence of information, including all the conditions needed to undersand the physical design, including lighting, material texture, color, scale, site and location, space, and architectural form.

The ability to transform an architectural design concept into an illustration appears magical, but, in reality, it originates with discipline of perception and repeated practice in sketching. Included in this book is a wide variety of preliminary studies, which provide a sampling of the images produced during the design process, including visual note taking, studies in line, tone, and texture, compositional studies and refinements, a survey of open and closed compositional designs, fully representative illustrations of urban and industrial projects, and the painter's response to traditional artistic subject matter and media. Their fine and seemingly effortless line work reflect the confidence of the artist in spontaneously composing elegant pictorial design. They subtly reveal the essence of architecture which comprises shaping the landscape and lending scale and human character to the environment, while at the same time, reveal the correspondence between abstraction and representation in drawing and architectural design.

RICHARD ROCHON
AMERICAN SOCIETY OF ARCHITECTURAL PERSPECTIVISTS

# About Bob Sutton

Robert L. Sutton (1924–85) used his sixty-one years creating beauty with his hands and making paint sing. An illustrator, architectural delineator, photographer, ceramist, and painter, he was, however, foremost a gifted artist who made ideas visible with his wonderful, expansive imagination. The works included in this book reflect his joy in translating ideas into beautifully descriptive pieces of art.

His works demonstrate the importance of visualizing and drawing. In any field of art—including architecture, illustration, interior design, product design, and landscape architecture—the process of understanding, conceptualizing, and portraying three-dimensional forms is challenging and deceptively difficult. In this regard, Sutton had exquisite talents.

Sutton visualized his clients' concepts, their dreams, and transcribed them into brilliant celebratory reality. Though he aspired to be a painter, he applied his talents primarily to advertising illustration and architectural delineation. Working in a variety of media—oil, transparent watercolor, acrylic, gouache, and casein—he would often do on-the-spot drawings of proposed buildings and interior environments before any final concepts had been developed.

He was born on February 24, 1924, in Connersville, Indiana, one of two sons of Esther and Cleo Sutton. At a young age, he drafted for his grandfather, a tool-and-die designer, doing mechanical drawing—immersed in the very different worlds of artistic and technical communication. He attended high school in Richmond, Indiana, and then the Meinsinger Art School in

Detroit before entering the army air corps (air force) during World War II. After the war Bob attended the Cincinnati Art Academy and apprenticed to local art studios and design offices. He married Nancy William in 1948 in Richmond, Indiana, and had two children, Ann Sutton Wiedlea and Scott Sutton.

His first place of employment in Detroit was the Smith, Hinchman and Grylls architectural firm. He later worked for a variety of local art studios and as a freelance advertising illustrator, before turning primarily to architectural illustration. He sometimes shared office space with others (such as the writer Elmore Leonard) but most often worked out of the third floor of his home in Birmingham, Michigan. Flying fascinated Bob throughout his life—he owned several airplanes over a twenty-year period. He also enjoyed ceramics, chess, and flying model airplanes with his son after he gave up flying.

Sutton was a recipient of the prestigious Bravo Award for illustration in 1963, given by the Art Directors Club of Detroit. His works are in corporate and private collections across the United States and have been displayed in national exhibitions such as the American Watercolor Society shows in New York. This book represents a sampling of Robert Sutton's large body of work, focusing upon his sketches specifically for architectural clientele. Many drawings and paintings are prominently displayed and remain in the collections of his clients around the world, in such places as Saudi Arabia, Thailand, and Hong Kong. Some are in unrecorded private collections, and others have been lost after having been reproduced.

# About Scott Sutton

His work has inspired almost everyone who knew him and requested his services. This book honors the memory of this man, his extraordinary talent and vision. It is our hope that as you view the work in this collection, Bob's ability to shape beauty may encourage and inspire you as well.

DON KERSTEN
PROFESSOR OF ART, UNIVERSITY OF MICHIGAN

Sadly, Scott Sutton died before this book was published. The son of the late Robert L. Sutton and husband of Patricia Burns Sutton, he was a leading architectural photographer in the midwestern United States. Like his father, he brought an exquisite eye to the photographic composition no matter what subject matter was involved. His works have been instrumental to many architectural firms who have used photographs to successfully enter design competitions, make client presentations, and prepare portfolios and promotional material. Scott's photographic architectural commissions appeared often in design publications such as the special edition of Better Homes and Gardens planned for the fall of 1992.

Scott's sensitivity to the visual world was due in part to growing up in a family of artists. His passion for visual exploration, however, originated from a youthful and creative imagination. His interest in photography was not limited to architecture, but included a wonderful portrait series of flowers and children, and a variety of sporting events, including professional speedboat racing, motorcycles, and airplanes in flight. In addition to a growing demand for his work by architectural offices, he received a steady flow of requests from around the country for his services as an accomplished pilot and aerial photographer.

# Introduction

A sketch is a form of graphic shorthand, a rough drawing that represents major features of an object in space. To be more specific, a sketch should convey the essence of a visual idea, simplify a complex subject, provide a pleasing abstract depiction of reality, express an idea with minimal line, tone, and texture, and serve as a spontaneous and quick method of representation (fig. I-1).

With few exceptions the sketches created by the late Robert L. Sutton in this book are efficient drawing/snapshots, recording moments of form, space, and light that may later have been rendered more thoroughly. Mastering the craft of sketching was of great significance to Sutton's evolution as an architectural illustrator. Rapid documentation and effective communication are the hallmarks of the accomplished sketch artist. Perhaps the key elements of drawing, which are also significant in Sutton's other works, are best expressed and mastered in sketching—proportion, perspective, composition, shade and shadow, and color (figs. I-2, I-3).

Sutton's ability to maintain a varied tone across an illustration while accentuating darks and lights lends enormous interest to his subjects. Not only are whites left bare to provide sparkle to the composition, but values are used sparingly overall to highlight the fine line of the pen stroke. No background (or very little) is used in many of these drawings because it could detract from the subject of the sketch.

The line strokes are important in these sketches; they not only suggest the materiality of form but also the material qualities of

I-1. The interior contrast of dark foliage against the white building pulls the attention of the viewer into and through the composition. Study drawing for ARCO Research Center, Philadelphia, Pennsylvania. Felt pen, designer's gouache and tone board. Giffels Associates, Inc.

the structure they represent. In the tradition of fine pencil and ink sketching by Andrew Loomis, Ernest Watson, and Theodore Kautzky, Sutton's sketches were created quickly, with an economy of tonal range, evocative in their simplicity and inclusive in the implication of all of the effects of detail and entourage (figs. I-4, I-5).

Sutton's reputation as a delineator encompassed a broad range of talents. One of the qualities most valued by architects was his facility with preliminary sketches or study drawings—that is, those drawings that act as a graphic metaphor to extend initial design concepts from the unknown toward three-dimensional reality. At first these sketches may seem to be articulate presentation drawings that adhere to formal graphic principles. Many, however, were quick, spontaneous sketches produced in the presence of a client. His ability to find an essential perspective

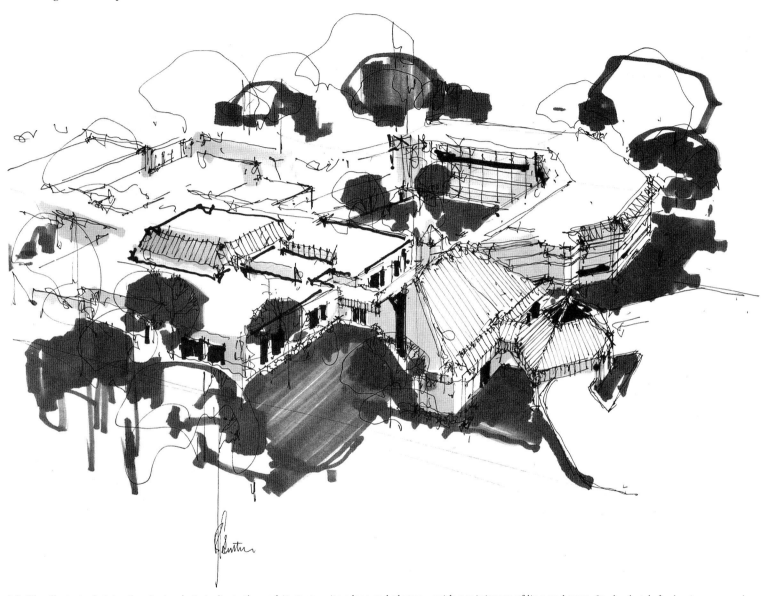

I-2. The illustrator's intention is simply to indicate the architecture—its edges and planes—with a minimum of line and tone. Study sketch for business complex. Felt pen on paper. Designer unknown.

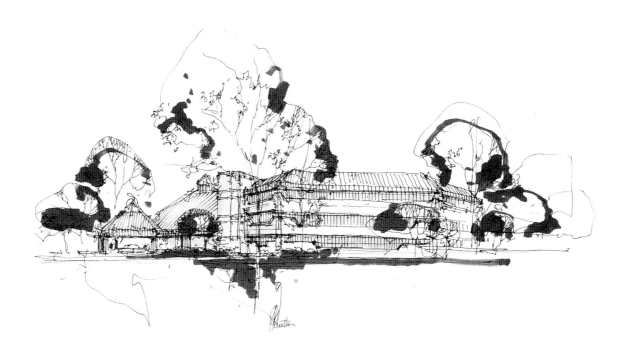

I-3. Nature is briefly detailed to help create a visual frame and reference of scale. Study sketch for business complex. Felt pen on paper. Designer unknown.

view that provided the most comprehensive orientation for depicting space while intuitively conveying a sense of scale could trigger a responsive chord in both designer and client.

Harry Vaporciyan, director of architecture at Giffels Associates, worked closely with Bob for approximately ten years, helping to cultivate Bob's skill in sketching immediate impressions of architectural concepts. Many of the design concepts originated by Harry and relayed to Bob for 3-D visualization resulted in some of the most fluid and free-flowing sketches that he created.

Many of these graphic impressions were used for discussion and design revision.

In a client's office, Bob's ability to sketch a view or spatial sequence quickly, taking the viewer into and through or around the concept was remarkable. Harry Vaporciyan remembers:

*Bob would visualize an architectural concept from beginning conversations. He began with what a form/space should feel like—the shape of the land and the space of the*

I-4. The free-flowing line work of trees in the vignetted composition complements the controlled detail of the architecture. Study sketch for Oakland University Library addition, Rochester, Michigan. Felt pen on paper. Rossetti Associates, Architects.

building in front of and to the sides—an expansive view subtly framed in a natural environment. Working without preconceived ideas of what things should look like, he invested his work with qualities of exploration, spontaneity, and improvisation. His fluid lines carry the eye into empty spaces—they draw together shapes of abstract shape somewhat cloudlike or treelike or human in form.

Bob could transform a design concept to provide a glimpse between realism and the abstract. He composed images with drama and visionary appeal, sometimes spending an hour on the main subject and another thirty minutes on the line that would rise above into the sky.

I-5. Study sketch for Oakland University Library addition, Rochester, Michigan. Felt pen on paper. Rossetti Associates, Architects.

Bob found innumerable influences in the commercial and fine arts, specifically illustration and painting. He admired the work of Andrew Wyeth, which encompassed fine illustration and painting; in his landscape painting in figure C-2, the treatment of composition, light, and form are comparable to Wyeth's in *Christina's World* (fig. C-1) and served as fertile ground for experimentation and fresh visual conception (fig. I-6).

One can speculate briefly on the influences of other illustrators on Bob's work. Marion Mahony Griffin, in collaboration with Frank Lloyd Wright, illustrated many beautiful portfolios in which vignetted composition and double or even triple studies on a single page reflect a Japanese influence (fig. I-7, C-3). Wright was attracted to the aesthetics of Japanese art, and he brought some of the compositional techniques of the Japanese print to

C-1. *Christina's World*. (1948) Andrew Wyeth. Tempera on gessoed panel, 32½" × 47¾". Collection. The Museum of Modern Art, New York. Purchase.

C-2. Landscape and barn. Acrylic and watercolor. Collection of the artist's family.

I-6. Barn study. Compositional exploration in watercolor, brush, and knife on paper. Collection of the artist.

the office rendering style. Griffin's rendering of Rock Crest/Rock Glen, Mason City, Iowa, as well as the elements of abstraction in the foliage and the flat areas of background composition, reflects an oriental influence. Similarly, several of Sutton's renderings of two images on a page reflect an awareness and sensitivity of line weight and economic use of white space, found in the Oriental traditions of drawing and printmaking (fig. I-8).

The highly decorative art of Helmut Jacoby may have also had appeal, not for its exacting detail but for his use of transparency, light, and atmosphere to make a strong visual statement (fig. C-4). Certainly, light, atmosphere, and reflection are main ingredients of Bob's illustration of the Grand Traverse Hotel and Resort Tower, designed by Redstone Associates, Architects (fig. C-5). And, during the 1950s, Robert E. Schwartz, one of the most successful practitioners in tempera paint, established a style that influenced countless young illustrators, including Sutton during his early career (figs. C-6, C-7).

Bob drew inspiration from the richness of established traditions in the arts and illustration. His education and apprenticeships exposed him to the lessons of history, media, and design composition, and he became a master of studio method and technique. He moved toward innovation through gesture drawing with line, tone, shape, and texture, maintaining a high degree of energy and imagination. The decision makers in architectural offices grew to trust this artist. As his contributions to design and art were well received, confidence in his own techniques became second nature (figs. I-9, I-10).

Bob shared a studio and office with the author Elmore ''Dutch'' Leonard for approximately ten years, where they casually discussed books, listened to each other's concerns, laughed easily, and shared the trials of artistic problems. Leonard has vivid memories of this period, as well as of several Sutton

paintings that eventually became part of Leonard's personal collection, which influenced the visual imagery in his books (fig. I-11). ''What impressed me so much about Bob's work was the way his foregrounds dominated the canvas in so many of his paintings. He created details in the foreground of what would be considered insignificant objects, while in the background a splash of color would indicate a barn or house.''

The elegance and supple manipulation of the vignetted composition demonstrated in many of Sutton's works, the control of light and scale, the expressive and spontaneous qualities of line and movement—these qualities are seldom seen in the work of other contemporary illustrators (fig. I-12). Many illustrators can bring forth a convincing vision of reality, impressive in technique, with a well-organized pictorial structure. However, not all illustrators or artists can create images with lasting appeal, haunting in their ability to stay in the mind, as Sutton did. With virtuosity came recognition by colleagues, peers, and professionals, signifying a status reserved only for those considered to be an artist's artist, an illustrator's illustrator. To the designer, he offered a clear and superior eye. To the student, he offers good examples of quick, clear sketching, to study and to ponder—what can be said visually in a few strokes of a pen or pencil can be just as persuasive and poetic as an illustration requiring several hours. Praised for his vision, his works are valued by many of the leading architectural firms and delineators across the country, especially in the Midwest where he lived and worked. Had he remained with us, certainly he would have witnessed this evidence of respect and admiration.

In a statement he drafted about his own rendering practice, he spoke of his job as an illustrator:

> *The scope of my service is somewhat limited to consideration of the practical use of color in pigment form—and*

C-3. Perspective rendering of Rock Crest/Rock Glen, Mason City, Iowa. Walter Burley Griffin and Marion Mahony Griffin, American partnership 1911–1937. Lithograph and gouache on green satin, c. 1912, 59 × 201 cm. Courtesy of The Art Institute of Chicago.

I-7. The World Fellowship Center, New Hampshire (1942). Marion Mahony Griffin. Ink on paper. Courtesy of The Art Institute of Chicago.

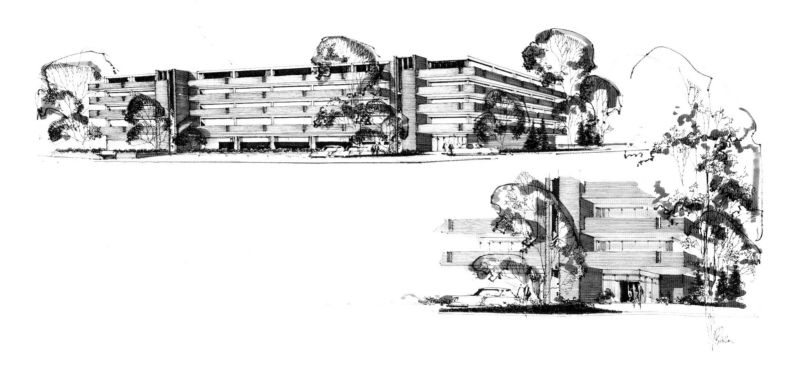

I-8. Double-page sketch study of an office complex includes a detail next to the full view in a vignetted composition. Pen-and-ink. Designer unknown.

C-4. Ford Foundation Headquarters, New York City. Helmut Jacoby. Ink and airbrush. Courtesy of Helmut Jacoby and the Ford Foundation.

C-5. Grand Traverse Hotel and Resort Tower. Watercolor on paper. Redstone Associates, Architects.

I-9. Sketch study created on site, drawn from observation. Bridge over Civic Center, Southfield, Michigan. Felt pen on paper. Giffels Associates, Inc.

particularly watercolor—in what is commonly termed representative painting.

My primary aim being to help in the solution of such problems of color representation as are peculiar to the architect and related areas of landscape and interior design. Not only do I make numerous preliminary studies, details

of ornament, color schemes for building materials, etc., but I am frequently faced with the difficult task of picturing on paper entire projects which are as yet merely proposed—buildings singly or in groups, landscape settings, interiors, and the like. Each of these projects, no matter how visionary, must be drawn so definitely and convincingly that the client or any layman concerned can see,

I-10. Sketch study created on site. Wayne County Jail and Bricktown, Detroit, Michigan. Felt pen on paper. Giffels Associates, Inc.

*before a contract is let, exactly how it will look when completed. And if such drawings are to be submitted to prospective clients, perhaps competitive (as they often are when new commissions are sought), they must be unusually attractive.*

*Presentation technique is of great significance. In terms of content, one of the things that eliminates a scheme or design concept is that its basic content does not come through clearly. I try to provide the greatest sense of comprehensive orientation for a space idea within a design*

C-6. Proposed Oklahoma City development. Robert E. Schwartz. Tempera. The Architectural League of New York. Pei Cobb Freed & Partners.

C-7. Energy resource recovery facility. Tempera. BEI Associates, Inc.

I-11. Composition with interior lights. Oil on canvas. Collection of Elmore Leonard.

concept. It is not merely plans, sections and elevations but rather scale, texture, color, and form.

As our old friend Vitruvius has said, "I have not studied with the view of making money by my profession: rather have I held that a slight fortune with good repute is to be pursued more than abounding wealth accompanied by disgrace."

As long as there are enough people in a profession who feel this way, outstanding work will be done.

I-12. The control of light and values attracts the eye. Study of Bristol-Myers Westwood Pharmaceuticals Research Center, Triangle Park, North Carolina. Felt pen and designer's gouache on tone board. Giffels Associates, Inc.

1-1. Sketching one view naturally raises questions about the design, which are explored in further drawings. Study sketch for architect's residence. Felt pen on paper. Designed by James Blain, Architect.

1-2. Sketch development includes nature and entourage. Study sketch for architect's residence. Felt pen on paper. Designed by James Blain, Architect.

# Part One:
# The Sketch Study

## Visual Note Taking

Much of the information in design is conveyed by sketching and graphic study. From the beginning of the design process, when doodlelike graphic explorations appear tentative and probing, through intermediate graphics, with their added detail, to final approvals that include highly detailed renderings and illustrations, the skill of the draftsperson in creating a graphic image when no solid, three-dimensional reality exists is a marvelous and often underestimated talent. As Raymond Myerscough-

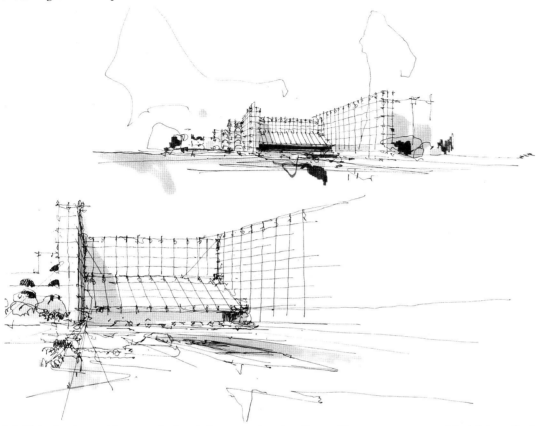

1-3. This sketch provides enough description to entice the client without locking the architect into a final design prematurely. Study sketch for proposed Middle East hospital entryway. Felt pen on paper. Giffels Associates, Inc.

Walker noted in his book *The Perspectivist*, ''The perspective as the drawing of a project not yet built is one of the few possibilities left to the three-dimensional painter with which the camera cannot possibly compete'' (figs. 1-1, 1-2).

It is important to note at the outset that the essence of a design concept is often conveyed through layer upon layer of sketched ideas and through a very simple and direct graphic rendition of form and space. An accurate line drawing that delineates an optimal amount of detail, portrays the design subject from an effective viewpoint, and presents the subject in an interesting fashion is the basis of coherent visual communication. Any further development of graphic imagery is elaboration, and embellishment of the design and illustration concept. Very often, designs were just beginning in the architectural office when Robert Sutton was hired. He included just enough description in his sketches to entice the client without locking the architect into a final design prematurely (figs. 1-3, 1-4).

1-4. A graphic impression provides a simple description and minimal detail. Study sketch for proposed Middle East hospital lobby on lower level. Felt pen on paper. Giffels Associates, Inc.

The ability to sketch with an economy of line, tone, color, and texture begins with exercises that train the eye to focus only on those visual elements of greatest importance to the subject. Capturing the most important elements in only a few lines and tones also trains the eye to visualize selectively, choosing the appropriate line weights, values, and colors for the construction of a visual environment. The ability to communicate a desired mood is achieved through many attempts at quickly grasping essential visual elements, which should be easily recognizable, expressed in spontaneous and unrehearsed drawings (figs. 1-5, 1-6, and 1-7).

Accurate and effective freehand perspective sketches are used in many preliminary stages of the design process. Preliminary sketch studies in design are often enhanced through simplification, learning to achieve maximum effect using minimum detail.

1-5. Strong, forceful values create drama and provide a simple description. Sketch proposal for International Market Place Entrance, Greektown, Detroit, Michigan. Felt pen on paper. BEI Associates, Inc.

One of the most important secrets: even the most complicated structure has basic, underlying patterns of shape, form, color, and texture that, individually or together, can form a simple visual pattern and establish the theme for a single sketch or series of explorations (figs. 1-8, 1-9).

## Sketchbooks

Paul Klee said that the way we perceive form is the way we perceive the world, and nowhere is this more evident and beautifully displayed than in a sketchbook. By introducing direct

1-6. The play of light and strong shadow provides depth in a simple graphic study. Sketch proposal for International Market Place, Detroit, Michigan. Felt pen on paper. BEI Associates, Inc.

1-7. Visual note·taking in simple drawings seems almost like handwriting. Study sketch for interior of International Market Place, Detroit, Michigan. Felt pen on paper. BEI Associates, Inc.

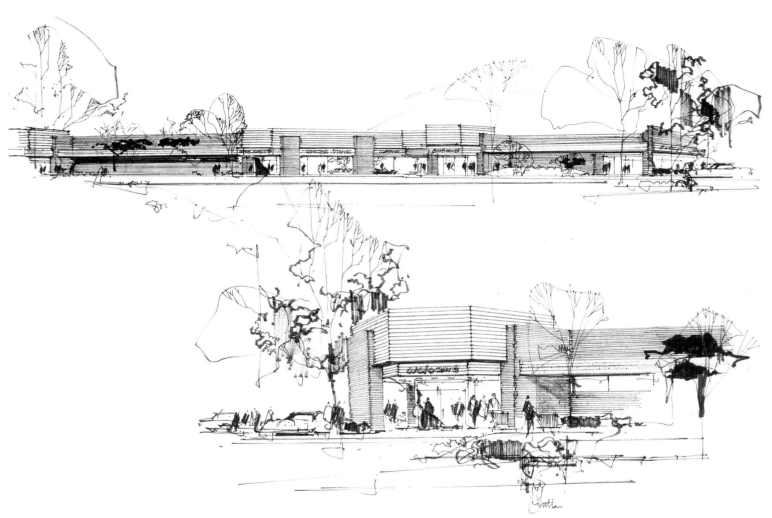

1-8. A visual pattern acts as a foil for the contrasting elements of trees, people, and cars. Study sketch for Harbor Point Plaza, Troy, Michigan. Felt pen on illustration board. Robert B. Alpern, Architect.

1-9. The sketch quality of the figures adds a sense of movement and transparency to the composition. Detail of Harbor Point Plaza, Troy, Michigan. Felt pen on illustration board. Robert B. Alpern, Architect.

1-10. A sketch exploration to discover visual avenues for further work. Early study sketch of Oakland University Library addition, Rochester, Michigan. Felt pen on paper. Rossetti Associates, Architects.

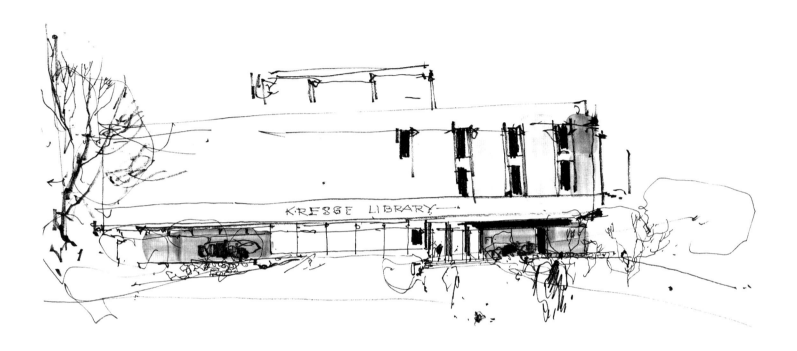

1-11. Sketch exploration to formulate ideas about the design and its illustration. Early study sketch of entrance to Oakland University Library addition, Rochester, Michigan. Felt pen on paper. Rossetti Associates, Architects.

experience into the making of art and illustration, the sketchbook plays a vital role, recording object observations from life that a designer can then use in the studio and office.

Sketchbooks are a means for juggling ideas and materials, as well as a practical place for self-instruction—a testing ground for ideas and formal design concerns. They are not intended to be final statements but directional signals that may lead to a new solution for an old problem (fig. 1-10).

It is impossible to develop every idea in a sketchbook into a sketch. Often written notes in the margin can act as future cues for a later, more developed drawing. Notations do not only save time but in the long run, become a reservoir of quickly conceived ideas which are often the most valid ones (fig. 1-11).

Sutton's drawing style is hasty, rapidly pushing toward a stated idea. Sometimes these studies lead simply to a series of sketch-

1-12. The strong contrast of this sketch study proposal conveys a light-filled courtyard. Interior courtyard of Texas Instruments, Inc. Research & Development/Manufacturing Facility, Denton, Texas. Felt pen on illustration board. Giffels Associates, Inc.

book drawings; sometimes more finished drawings are made after his ideas have been firmly established, as in figure 1-12.

A sketchbook is a repository or memory bank for information and feelings that may escape if left unrecorded. A fleeting thought shimmering in the mind's eye can lead to new ideas when it is seen later from a fresh perspective. Although many designers use the sketchbook for serious studies only, playful improvisation is just as significant. Sutton's fascination with flight, airplanes, and aerial views provided impetus for many vantage points in his drawings. The fanciful geometric forms and spaces of architectural design are made even more dramatic by his ability to picture the viewer's response to seeing the building from various points above and around the structure (figs. 1-13, 1-14, 1-15, and 1-16).

1-13. Aerial view—a vertical pattern of sketched strokes implies the shimmering quality of light. Study sketch of entrance of Town Center Development, Southfield, Michigan. Felt pen on paper. Solomon, Cordwell, Buenz and Associates, Inc.

Regardless of its form—as a bound book or a series of pages to be bound later—a sketchbook functions as a source of ideas, providing direction for new work. Working from a sketchbook enables you to expand upon ideas that have a history—you have done some thinking about them already. Providing the benefit of time and a different viewpoint, working from a sketchbook encourages the evolution of an idea to a satisfying maturity; the momentum of *process* and *progress*—returning to an idea that has inspired you once, to build upon that inspiration—aids in that development. Over the years sketchbooks become a valuable resource, tracing one's growth as an artist. Among all of one's travels and life experiences, sketching acts as a deeply personal reminder of information and relationships.

1-14. The massing of foliage encompasses the space and subtly frames the vignetted aerial illustration. Study sketch of ground floors of Town Center Development, Southfield, Michigan. Felt pen on paper. Solomon, Cordwell, Buenz and Associates, Inc.

## Line, Tone, and Texture

Beyond the formal process of perception in sketching lies the dynamic human activity of translating, interpreting, and storing information. Transforming real images into drawn symbols involves three stages: identification, simplification, and expression. Sketching, as a reflex action, includes drawing what you see or what you know.

The formative lines (as exemplified by the linework in the sketches in this book) identify and define the specific character of the subject matter—its visual and physical qualities of form.

1-15. The strong contrast between forceful vertical and horizontal strokes lends a sense of volume to the buildings in this aerial view. Study sketch of Town Center Development, Southfield, Michigan. Felt pen on paper. Solomon, Cordwell, Buenz and Associates, Inc.

1-16. Volumes are communicated with simple lines, tones, and textures. Study sketch of condominium at Town Center Development, Southfield, Michigan. Felt pen on paper. Solomon, Cordwell, Buenz and Associates, Inc.

1-17. Space is communicated with simple lines, tones, and textures. Study sketch of interior of Town Center shopping arcade, Southfield, Michigan. Felt pen on paper. 3D International.

Further classification of the visual field into foreground, middle ground, and background, in coordination with tonal contrast and light source, conveys the spatial arrangement and establishes the compositional structure of a drawing.

As important as the visual elements is the use of perspective, including an appropriate station point and eye level. At the

beginning of the sketch, the most significant rays (lines of perspective construction) are established in a somewhat relaxed manner, lending partial definition to the design concept (fig. 1-17). Darker linework, a wash of gray, and textural effects can be introduced in an open composition, where the definition of shapes and volumes is created gradually over the drawing field (fig. 1-18). Selecting various viewpoints around the subject

1-18. The impression of an arcade is created with a few lines. Study of street-level arcade in the Marquette Building, Detroit, Michigan. Felt pen on paper. Giffels Associates, Inc.

exercises the ability to handle perspectives while training the eye to isolate concentrated design elements from a busy environment (fig. 1-19). Beyond the mechanics of perspective construction, the role of station point is also an important aesthetic decision, providing space around the subject for the development of vistas and appropriate entourage. For similar reasons establishing an appropriate eye level—giving equal space above and below the design or giving dominance to one or the other—is a question of aesthetic choice (fig. 1-20).

The value concept is one of the essential ingredients of a sketch, distinguishing the pattern of light and form and establishing the overall mood of the illustration (figs. 1-21, 1-22). Striving for an economy of means—using the minimal number of values, that

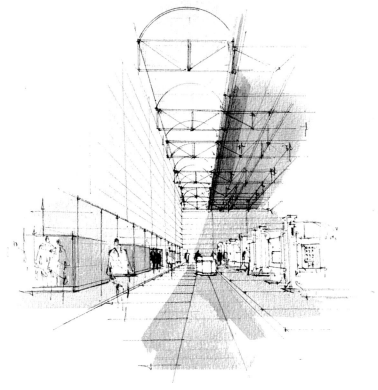

1 19. The impression of an interior passageway is conveyed by a few lines of constructed perspective. Study sketch of interior of Federal Mogul Corporation Ball Bearing Plant, Lititz, Pennsylvania. Felt pen on paper. Giffels Associates, Inc.

is, light, middle, and dark—is helpful in constructing the most basic value pattern; the light value can be either the white of the drawing paper or a very light gray tone (fig. 1-23). The design concept conveyed through a minimum of three values is a basic structure, working to maintain the visual plan and development of the subject matter within its setting (fig. 1-24).

The selection of values or color suggests a relationship between what is observed and what is established in a pictorial space. A high-key color concept is established with predominantly light values, a low-key range (with dominant dark values) appears dark overall, and a middle-key concept suggests the use of dark and light values with middle grays dominating. The choice of a full range of values for a sketch or more elaborate drawing establishes atmosphere and lighting, which in turn should be followed consistently in a study or final illustration (fig. 1-25).

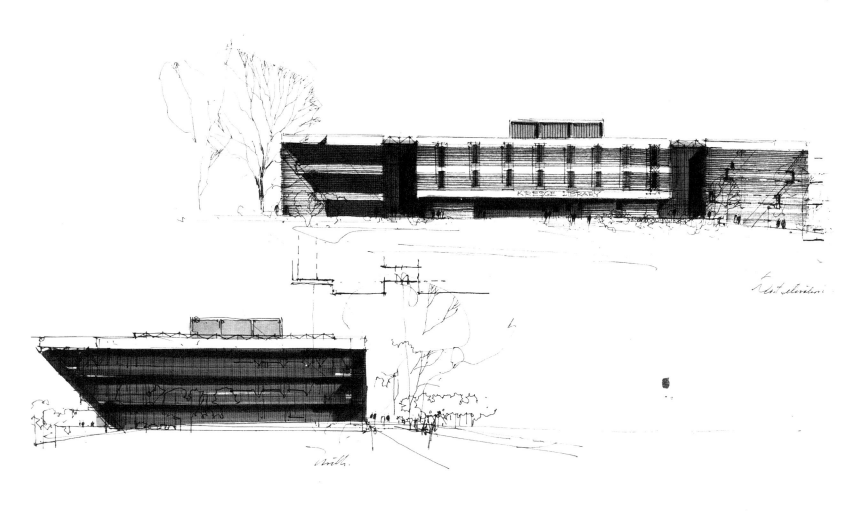

1-20. One view leads to the understanding and development of the other views. Elevation studies of Oakland University Library addition, Rochester, Michigan. Felt pen on paper. Rossetti Associates, Architects.

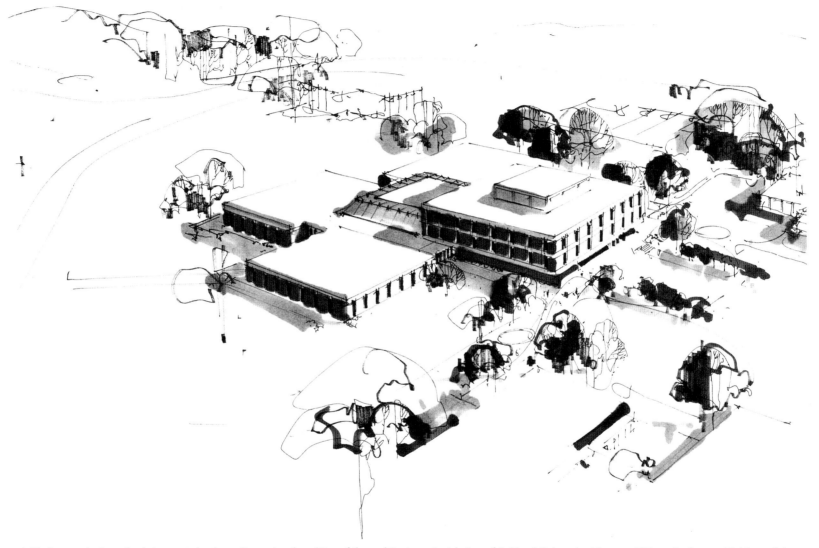

1-21. Strong shadow play brings out the three-dimensional qualities of the architecture. Aerial view of Oakland University Library addition, Rochester, Michigan. Felt pen on paper. Rossetti Associates, Architects.

1-22. The value concept creates a sense of strong sunlight and crisp shadow. Perspective view of Oakland University Library addition, Rochester, Michigan. Felt pen on paper. Rossetti Associates, Architects.

1-23. The value concept is heavily emphasized in the fenestration of the library building. Close-up perspective view of Oakland University Library addition, Rochester, Michigan. Felt pen on paper. Rossetti Associates, Architects.

1-24. A high-contrast study of the library and its entourage. Driveway view of Oakland University Library addition, Rochester, Michigan. Felt pen on paper. Rossetti Associates, Architects.

1-25. A wider range of values provides more opportunity for detail. View of Crystal Palace Casino shopping mall, Nassau, Bahamas. Felt pen on paper. BEI Associates, Inc.

Variation in the qualities of illumination lend visual interest and excitement to a sketch. Some of the most effective sketches are considered impressionistic because of their subtle representation of illumination and careful modulation of value and color. Sketching the effects of a number of lighting conditions, such as dappled, striking, reflective, intense, or luminescent, establishes surface patterns of interest in addition to illuminating objects and environments. Included here are several studies and details that convey many of these lighting conditions and exemplify how the treatment of illumination can enhance an architectural form (fig. 1-26).

1-26. Softened contrast within an interior space is communicated by a wider range of gray values. Interior perspective view of Crystal Palace shopping mall. Felt pen on paper. BEI Associates, Inc.

1-27. The shimmering quality of the grays results from the spacing of the dark lines and light background. Perspective view of hotel entrance. Felt pen on paper. Designer unknown.

Sketching involves more than lines and shading, and the act of making marks in sketching will fascinate those who enjoy experimenting with drawing tools and graphic media. There are an infinite number of ways to achieve texture with markers, ink pens, brushes, and supporting studio equipment. Often not only the tool, but how it is used—fast or slow, textural stippling or dragging it across a surface at an angle—will produce various effects. Experimenting with pointed marks and linear marks improves one's ability to produce natural or man-made textures with an economy of means in many improvisational situations. Figures 1-27, 1-28, 1-29, and 1-30 demonstrate how a pen can be used in various ways to sketch landscapes and architectural environments.

1-28. The massing of lines creates a focal point and provides contrast at the center of the composition. Interior perspective view of hotel lobby. Felt pen on paper. Designer unknown.

## Composition and Refinements

The art of composition—bringing order to the various graphic elements that make up a design—is both intuitive and conscious. The arrangement of form in space and the illustrator's visual sense of design are important factors in laying out a subject for an illustration and resolving any problems that occur. In many instances, the center of interest in architectural illustration is a building, a group of buildings, or an interior view. Making the main subject prominent but not overwhelming is an artistic problem with many aesthetic solutions (figs. 1-31, 1-32).

1-29. Sparkle is created by alternating light and dark depictions of the hotel floors and lobby. Interior lobby, aerial view, of hotel. Felt pen on paper. Designer unknown.

1-30. The use of man-made and natural textures creates a complementary juxtaposition. Exterior perspective study of hotel. Felt pen on paper. Designer unknown.

1-31. The relationship of two illustrations on a single sheet is enhanced through vignetted composition and the interplay of natural forms. Perspective studies for Brentwood Medical Center, Livonia, Michigan. Felt pen on paper. Robert B. Alpern, Architect.

1-32. Interest in nature is emphasized to enhance the sheet design of an architectural illustration. Detail of Brentwood Medical Center, Livonia, Michigan. Robert B. Alpern, Architect.

The illustrator is clearly interested in achieving balance across the compositional field. Such factors as value range, line weights, the use of white space, and the concise definition of form and space all contribute to a hierarchy of visual interest and are therefore important in the successful orchestration of the picture. Additionally, proportion—the relation of the whole of the composition to the size of the paper, as well as the relation of the subject and its size to other objects in the picture—is of main interest. The treatment and organization of all the visual elements should complement and support the building illustration (figs. 1-33, 1-34).

The use of several line qualities, from delicate to coarse, can create a hierarchy of visual interest, lending the greatest emphasis to the subject or center of interest. Developing one's visual sensitivity for the effective use of blank or white space adds an important dimension of subtlety to a composition, as does the

1-33. Detail and texture are carefully positioned and related within the sheet composition. Perspective views of Bonaventure Skating and Mall, Farmington Hills, Michigan. Felt pen on paper. Robert B. Alpern, Architect.

1-34. Interest is created above and below the architectural elements. The darkest contrast brings the eye back to the center of the composition after viewing the surround. Detail of Bonaventure Skating and Mall, Farmington Hills, Michigan. Robert B. Alpern Architect.

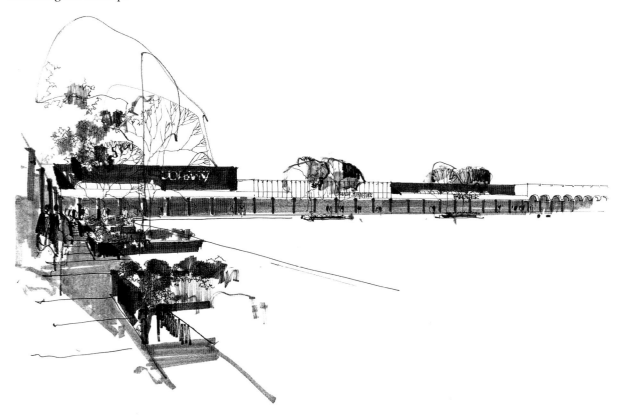

1-35. The effective use of negative space complements the interest created in the foreground and background. Exterior perspective study of Northwood Shopping Center, Royal Oak, Michigan. Felt pen on paper. Robert B. Alpern, Architect.

use of concentrated detail across the entire sheet. A brevity of stroke along with the concise definition of form and space reflect the intention of simplicity in illustration, an economy of means, especially in ink and marker sketching (figs. 1-35, 1-36).

It is interesting to note that the better we understand pictures the more we recognize the common graphic language with which they communicate. Regardless of their complexity, illustrations are based on this common language, even in totally different cultures. Composition, like chess, depends upon the way the game is played rather than upon the elegance of the individual pieces. Once understood, the arrangement of shapes and forms may be conveyed in more complex and highly refined graphic terms. Often, of course, the more mature the artist, the more simple and subtle his or her statement becomes.

1-36. Transparency in the depiction of nature and entourage adds visual movement and animates the composition. Detail of Northwood Shopping Center, Royal Oak, Michigan. Felt pen on paper. Robert B. Alpern, Architect.

1-37. The foliage and the building retain their own identities while supporting the entire composition. Sketch study of the entrance for Design Center of the Americas, Davie, Florida. Pen-and-ink (preliminary study). Robert B. Alpern, Architect.

Whether using a bird's-eye view of a building or the more common eye-level height above or below the subject, it is important that the viewpoint be natural, credible, and practical. In the case where a long, low building stretches across the drawing field, the use of natural subject matter as entourage, such as landscape elements, people, and geographic elements, can help frame the composition to the left and right, giving different emphasis to each. The design principles of unity and balance are vital to the success of any illustration; equilibrium results when each element of an illustration, including the main interest area, retains its own identity but supports the whole composition. If too many contrasts exist within the subject or in

1-38. Simple contrasts in the sketch maintain unity and a single focal point. Study of garden court, Design Center of the Americas, Davie, Florida. Felt pen on paper (preliminary study). Robert B. Alpern, Architect.

its design and style of illustration, the composition will be unbalanced and will therefore lack unity (figs. 1-37, 1-38, 1-39, and 1-40).

## Critical Evaluation

After creating the sketch and allowing enough time to understand and respond to it, an illustrator evaluates it. Posing relevant questions often results in appropriate insight that can be incorporated into the work. For example, does the sketch convey what you intended? Does it bring to light other important issues? Do questions about the illustrator's intent and what is reflected in the drawing remain? Can you change the form to enhance or clarify meaning? Try to differentiate between the intent of a form and its meaning. If form is a vehicle for meaning, what is the message to you, the viewer? Very often the best illustrators are their own harshest critics. They have become somewhat accus-

1-39. When a long, low building stretches across the drawing field, natural subject matter can help frame the composition. Perspective view of parking and driveway, Design Center of the Americas, Davie, Florida. Felt pen on paper (preliminary study). Robert B. Alpern, Architect.

tomed to posing and answering tough questions about issues affecting their work. Above and beyond this internal dialog of critical evaluation, it is important to go with your feelings about the work. If you feel dissatisfied without knowing why, consider these five categories when trying to identify the problem:

- Inconsistent graphic method or mood
- Difficulty in organizing a basic visual pattern
- Disregard for the relationship of positive form and negative space
- Underdeveloped gradations of value and color
- Inaccurate observation

1-40. A normal eye-level view is natural, credible, and practical. Perspective view of parking, Design Center of the Americas, Davie, Florida. Robert B. Alpern, Architect.

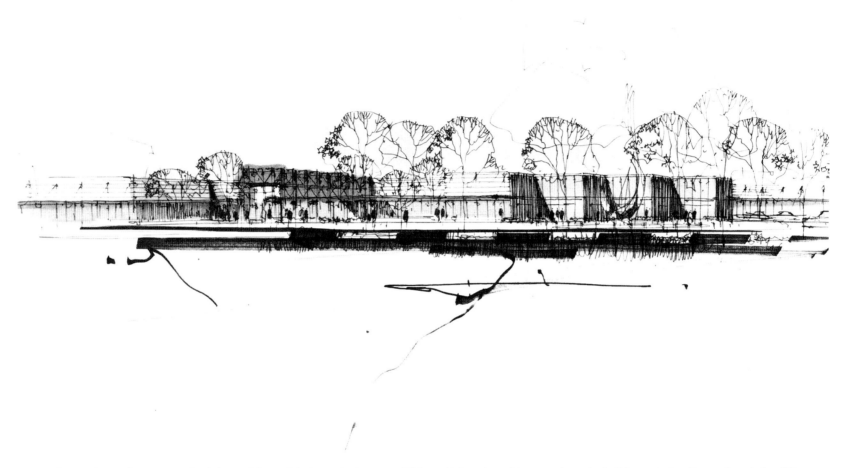

2-1. The simplicity of massing and a light, middle, and dark tonal scheme establish multiple points of interest along the building exterior. Perspective study of Texas Instruments Inc. Research & Development/Manufacturing Facility, Denton, Texas. Felt pen on paper. Giffels Associates, Inc.

2-2. One heightened detail at the entryway establishes a focal point in the illustration. Perspective study of Texas Instruments Inc. Research & Development/ Manufacturing Facility, Denton, Texas. Felt pen on paper. Giffels Associates, Inc.

# Part Two:
# Thematic Drawings

The widely published drawing styles of modern architects, such as Le Corbusier, Eero Saarinen, and Frank Lloyd Wright, and delineators, such as J. Henderson Barr and Helmut Jacoby, are internationally well known. Less known, however, is the function of drawing within the design process. In many offices high priority is rarely given to graphics that depict finished architecture as a built event. Rather, much greater emphasis is given to drawings that represent the essential spirit of a design concept.

From the beginning of a project, a profusion of drawings focuses on embryonic ideas in three-dimensional form (figs. 2-1, 2-2, and 2-3). Projected from freehand plans, elevations, and models, they are often drawn in ink, marker, or graphite on tracing paper. At this stage color is used simply, if at all, and only to describe surface appearance or highlight form and intensify the three-dimensional illusion of the graphics. A basic three-dimensional approach that allows the problem of shape and massing to be addressed at an early stage—often in black-and-white—has a neutralizing effect on all but the emphasis of architectural form.

2-3. Vertical elements contrast with the low horizontal lines of the building to lend focus to the entrance. Perspective of drive and entrance of Texas Instruments, Inc. Research & Development/Manufacturing Facility, Denton, Texas. Felt pen on paper. Giffels Associates, Inc.

2-4. The layering of line qualities establishes a strong perspective view, lighting, and texture. Early sketch of bridge, GMISCA building at General Motors Technical Center, Warren, Michigan. Felt pen on paper. Giffels Associates, Inc.

## Study Groupings

The initial graphic modeling of a developing three-dimensional concept can include small-scale models. However, the most significant development begins with a sequence of prophetic doodles that act to crystallize the designer's initial response to the scheme (fig. 2-4). These small pencil, marker, or ink drawings also act as an iconic and continuous point of reference throughout the design process. They identify a clear structural diagram, comprising the profile of a form, such as a central arch, as seen from an important vantage point, and can establish the main design statement at a very early stage. In doing so, they trigger a chain of evolving drawings and provide a kind of checklist against which ensuing thematic variations can be

2-5. An aerial view through a window frames the focal point (Cobo Hall), depicted in greater detail. View to Cobo Hall from the Marquette Building, Detroit, Michigan. Felt pen on paper. Giffels Associates, Inc.

2-6. The foil of a dark backdrop clarifies every detail. Design proposal of Giffels Office Building, Southfield, Michigan. Felt pen on paper. Giffels Associates, Inc.

tested, and they exert a powerful influence over all other aspects of the developing architectural form (fig. 2-5).

Thematic drawings, which by definition have an image or idea in common, usually take the form of an extended group of works. Illustrators have always worked in thematically related series, but the recent preoccupation with process, materials, and design evolution make the sketch series all the more common today (figs. 2-6, 2-7).

There are several reasons to develop a series or group of images on a single page. A most basic reason is that illustration involves the mind and coordination between the eye and hand. From experimentation with thinking to active involvement in doing, or vice versa, the emphasis shifts to process rather than product. Since the drawing series is an open-ended experience, there are opportunities to compare one image with another and to express more variations on a single idea than in just one work. Nothing can better illustrate the number of compositional and stylistic

2-7. Transparency and reflection are achieved through the mingling of dark vertical lines and a gray ground. Design proposal of lobby for Giffels Office Building, Southfield, Michigan. Felt pen on paper. Giffels Associates, Inc.

variations possible on a given subject than Sutton's thematic drawings showing proposals for United Technologies's meeting rooms and cafeteria in figures 2-8 and 2-9.

Work can be investigated more deeply in study groupings than in a single image. Often shared themes become the means by which an illustrator joins his or her concept of form with the client's interests in an established subject (figs. 2-10, 2-11, and 2-12). Needless to say, personal themes are a valuable resource to an illustrator but are more appropriate to the artist's private work and are therefore discussed in the final part of this book.

2-8. The drawing series is an open-ended experience, enabling the comparison of one image to another. Studies of United Technologies's Pratt & Whitney Jet Engine Rebuild Facility meeting room and office, Southington, Connecticut. Felt pen on paper. Giffels Associates, Inc.

2-9. A single idea can include numerous variations. Study of cafeteria for United Technologies's Pratt & Whitney Jet Engine Rebuild Facility. Southington, Connecticut. Felt pen on paper. Giffels Associates, Inc.

2-10. Shared themes become the means by which an illustrator joins a concept with the client's interests in an established subject. Double-page study of exterior and interior lobby of Design Center, Troy, Michigan. Pen-and-ink on paper. Robert B. Alpern, Architect.

2-11. Study groupings allow a closer investigation of a subject than a single sketch can. Exterior perspective study of American Child prototype plan, Dallas, Texas. Felt pen on illustration board. Robert B. Alpern, Architect.

2-12. Interior spaces seem to flow into one another in a study grouping. Interior perspective study of American Child prototype plan. Felt pen on illustration board. Robert B. Alpern, Architect.

2-13. Graphic conceptualization is given priority over drawing refinements. Entrance study of Queen of Heaven Cemetery, New Baltimore, Pennsylvania. Felt pen on paper. Harley Ellington Pierce Yee Associates, Inc.

## Studies Extended

In much of Sutton's work, the emphasis is not on a polished, finished drawing but rather on an idea, a design concept and its environment (figs. 2-13, 2-14). The drawings are energetic, sometimes with just enough detail to convey the idea. Sutton chose a specific geographical site for every design concept, and each enhanced the other (figs. 2-15, 2-16, 2-17, and 2-18).

Sutton's themes were so well appreciated by his audience and clientele that knowledge of other illustrators' works and styles was not necessary for the viewer to appreciate them (fig. 2-19). Such themes appealed to a wide audience of designers. Sutton's inspiration often resulted from thinking about transformations. His experimentation with scale and viewpoint in an analytical approach transformed the visual aspects of the objects and spaces (figs. 2-20, 2-21, and 2-22). Analyzing the function of the

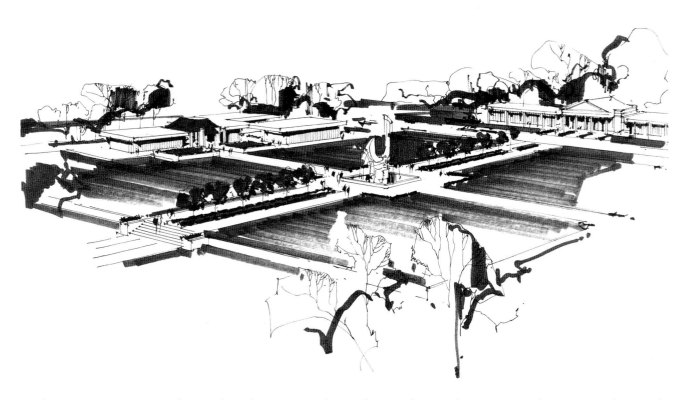

2-14. The concept is constructed in simple graphic terms. Aerial view of Queen of Heaven Cemetery, New Baltimore, Pennsylvania. Felt pen on paper. Harley Ellington Pierce Yee Associates, Inc.

object under various conditions can also produce leaps of imagination and associations. Giving architecture anthropomorphic characteristics can dramatically or subtly affect the shape, form, and space.

Similarly, changes to the landscape, that is, natural forms and textures, affect composition from drawing to drawing (figs. 2-23, 2-24, 2-25, 2-26, 2-27, and 2-28). The development of expressive content over a group of drawings does not exclude a subjective approach but rather assumes that the various forms of graphic experimentation combine to make a unified statement. Each drawing in a series will suggest new ideas for succeeding drawings. Illustrators observe, distinguish, and relate.

2-15. The inclusion of the setting expands the reality of the design concept. Perspective view through walkway of Oakland University Library addition, Rochester, Michigan. Felt pen on paper. Rossetti Associates, Inc.

2-16. The setting acts as a visual entrance. Perspective view of Oakland University Library addition, Rochester, Michigan. Felt pen on paper. Rossetti Associates, Inc.

2-17. Setting also softens the appearance of architectonic form. View from the driveway of Oakland University Library addition, Rochester, Michigan. Felt pen on paper. Rossetti Associates, Inc.

2-18. Setting offers opportunities to express entourage and accentuate the design concept. Alternate view of drive of Oakland University Library addition, Rochester, Michigan. Felt pen on paper. Rossetti Associates, Inc.

2-19. Soft impressionistic vignette study with light and dark linear tones. Perspective sketch of hotel entrance. Felt pen on paper. Designer unknown.

2-20. Experimentation with viewpoint adds interest to the entire design, not just the building. Study of the entrance drive to IBM Research Complex, East Fishkill, New York. Pen-and-ink on paper. BEI Associates, Inc.

2-21. Experimentation with context and scale adds interest to the design. Study of IBM Research Complex, East Fishkill, New York. Pen-and-ink on paper. BEI Associates, Inc.

2-22. Familiar visual aspects of the architecture and its environment. Perspective study of IBM Research Complex, East Fishkill, New York. Pen-and-ink on paper. BEI Associates, Inc.

2-23. Various forms of graphic expression combine to make a unified statement. Proposal for King Fahd International Terminal, Saudi Arabia. Eastern Providence Royal Terminal Project. Felt pen on paper. Yamasaki and Associates.

2-24. The important conceptual idea dominates the composition. Study of terminal interior, proposal for King Fahd International Terminal, Saudi Arabia. Felt pen on paper. Yamasaki and Associates.

2-25. Deep shadows and light impart a great spatial quality to the concept. Study of exterior terminal and jet, proposal for King Fahd International Terminal, Saudi Arabia. Felt pen on paper. Yamasaki and Associates.

2-26. Imagery appropriate to the concept complements the illustration. Study of exterior terminal and jet, proposal for King Fahd International Terminal, Saudi Arabia. Felt pen on paper. Yamasaki and Associates.

2-27. Graphic experimentation with the spatial arrangement from drawing to drawing adds interest to the concept. Overview sketch of terminal and connecting walkways, proposal for King Fahd International Terminal, Saudi Arabia. Felt pen on paper. Yamasaki and Associates

2-28. Each drawing contributes to the development of an overall idea. Aerial view of terminal, proposal for King Fahd International Terminal, Saudi Arabia. Felt pen on paper. Yamasaki and Associates.

3-1. A relatively small illustration executed in the middle of a large sheet of paper floats on the sheet, unaffected by the empty surround. Aerial study of cable television station. Pen-and-ink with felt pen. Designer unknown.

3-2. An illustration surrounded by blank space is called a spot drawing or vignette composition. Perspective study of cable television station. Pen-and-ink with felt pen. Designer unknown.

# Part Three: Compositional Schemes

Many of Robert Sutton's illustrations navigated between the pure definitions of open and closed composition to explore the nature of illustration design. Open and closed designs can be equally effective artistic devices in the construction of visual composition. In this part these design principles will be discussed.

In the search for picture control, one of the first experiments should be to learn to see a spot on the surface not as a symbol of something in nature but as a disturbance in theoretical space—in a depth environment not associated with an actual space as experienced in nature. This visual facility as exercised in

3-3. The impressionistic use of white space acts as an illustrative element forming the surrounding space. Proposal drawing for private residence. Felt pen on paper. Designer unknown.

perception is truly the beginning of perceiving graphic space. As fantastic as it seems, this emptiness or void is an important dimension in pictorial design that must be grasped before a successful pictorial structure can be developed. As long as we see the spot as simply a geometric shape within the context of a geometric drawing field, the relevance of pictorial design will remain a mystery (fig. 3-1).

## Open and Closed Designs

Many renowned fine and commercial artists create works that use an impressionistic white, or blank, space in areas surrounding the subject matter (fig. 3-2). If the size and shape of the drawing surface is of little or no importance in the layout, design, and construction of an illustration, the picture is usually called an *open* composition. For example, a relatively small illustration executed in the middle of a relatively large drawing

3-4. Vignetted compositions can be quite natural. View of residence entrance. Felt pen on paper. Designer unknown.

sheet is little influenced by the edges of the paper and therefore appears to float on the sheet, unaffected by the empty surround. These compositions are sometimes called spot drawings or vignettes (figs. 3-3, 3-4, 3-5, and 3-6).

When borders limit the size and shape of an illustration, it is usually referred to as a *closed* picture. The borders can be created by the artist, or the limit can be imposed by the edges of the drawing surface, in technical terms a *bleed* (figs. 3-7, 3-8).

The many degrees of variation between open and closed pictorial design hold creative possibilities for the composition of beautiful illustrative subject matter. Focusing the imagination on the possibilities of the pictorial space on the page can lead to a myriad of new constructions of space-form composition.

3-5. The many degrees of variation between open and closed pictorial design offer creative possibilities. Interior perspective study of International Market Place, Greektown, Detroit, Michigan. Felt pen on paper. BEI Associates, Inc.

3-6. A vignette composition subtly framed at the sides by natural forms. Interior study of International Market Place, Greektown, Detroit, Michigan. Felt pen on paper. BEI Associates, Inc.

3-7. When the edges act as borders, the result is a closed picture. Proposal drawing of International Market Place, Greektown, Detroit, Michigan. Felt pen on illustration board. BEI Associates, Inc.

## Cropping

Cropping, a term used extensively in still photography, implies a control of space essential to achieve legibility. Cropping means to reduce the amount of area of a visual image by adjusting its border. Usually when an important element is made tangent to a

3-8. An illustration covering an entire surface of limited dimensions is a closed picture. Entrance study of International Market Place, Greektown, Detroit, Michigan. Felt pen on illustration board. BEI Associates, Inc.

3-9. An important element, trees, made tangent to the top and right side. Perspective study of Michigan Bell Telephone Company Branch Facility, Detroit, Michigan. Felt pen on paper. Harley Ellington Pierce Yee and Associates, Inc.

border through improper cropping, a congestion arises that attracts the eye again and again (fig. 3-9). Eye movement and center of interest can be altered subtly or dramatically by reducing one or more of the picture dimensions (fig. 3-10). A subject cropped on all four sides may be made spacious by careful planning of the points of tension implied by the pictorial structure and subject matter.

## Entries and Exits

The theory of how the eye enters or exits a composition is controversial. Many artists feel that the idea of a point of entry is contradicted immediately by a picture's center of interest, where the greatest amount of contrast and unique form are usually found. The weakness to this argument is that it negates the

3-10. The center of interest is altered by a reduction in picture size. Perspective study of Michigan Bell Telephone Company Branch Facility, Detroit, Michigan. Felt pen on paper. Harley Ellington Pierce Yee and Associates, Inc.

notion that pictorial borders greatly affect the eye's view of the interior.

Another approach suggests that the eye enters a picture from the bottom, moving up to the center of interest, because the foreground, at the bottom, is closer to the viewer than middle ground or background. The use of perspective at the bottom of a picture, however, can overpower the remaining elements of composition. If additional elements of contrast at the point of entry are not included to balance strong perspective lines, the composition of a picture may seem awkward (fig. 3-11).

A third theory suggests that we see elements of a picture indiscriminately. This idea precludes the notion that a controlled

3-11. The additional elements of nature act as a foil for strong perspective lines. Perspective study of interior of Middle East hospital lobby. Felt pen on paper. Giffels Associates, Inc.

time pattern has any effect on guiding the eye into and out of pictorial subject matter. The application of this theory to a picture design would likely result in either an overly structured center of interest or visual chaos throughout.

Countless artists and illustrators have successfully used these hypotheses for many years. The rationale for structural theory in composition is inclusive of all constructive measures toward designing the picture. Along with directing the eye of the viewer through a pictorial structure, another controlling factor, which is often unseen, is atmospheric and graphic space (fig. 3-12, C-8, and C-9).

3-12. Points of interest are created along the ground plane. Study of main entrance for a Middle East hospital. Felt pen on paper. Giffels Associates, Inc.

C-8. Entrance study. Felt pen. Designer unknown.

C-9. Office interior and entrance. Pen-and-sepia-ink. Designer unknown.

3-13. A repeated rephrasing and description of volumes suggests three-dimensional forms. Building darkness against the white structure heightens the drama of the sketch study of ARCO Research Center, Philadelphia, Pennsylvania. Felt pen and designer's gouache on tone board. Giffels Associates, Inc.

## Atmospheric and Graphic Space

Through the careful adjustment of light-to-dark values in a drawing or painting, it is possible to alter the effects of form and space. When an atmospheric effect is dominant, the viewer confuses the distance separating forms in nature or volumes in a picture with space. When volumes and shapes are clearly present but submerged in the tonal structure of, say, a rainy-day effect, the surfaces of these forms become secondary to the overall surface of the total work. Just as the nineteenth-century impressionists immersed their subject matter in a sea of color and light, an atmospheric effect communicates not the reality of space but the feeling of forces in nature that take precedence over a portrayal of factual events.

3-14. A strong sense of graphic space is partly due to strong surface control. Wide perspective study of ARCO Research Center, Philadelphia, Pennsylvania. Felt pen and designer's gouache on tone board. Giffels Associates, Inc.

Sutton's ability to generate a strong sense of graphic space in his drawing is due in measure to his refined ability to maintain strong surface control. This is not to suggest that his works relied upon an organization of flat shapes but rather, a continual rephrasing and description of volumes suggesting three-dimensional forms, as seen in figures 3-13 and 3-14. One can see how such volumes have been translated in terms of perspective, rather than in terms of modeling and rendering. Curiously, it is through the realization of three-dimensional form that the evolution of original graphic shape is possible (figs. C-10, C-11). As these works show, the symbol of a figure is abstracted into a strong graphic structure, usually producing an exciting shape statement. To arrive at convincing abstractions of volumes in graphic space, the artist confronts problems involving such intangible factors as tension, movement, and shape impact—all of which can be mastered with constant and unending practice.

C-10. Commercial complex. Pen-and-sepia-ink. Designer unknown.

C-11. Apartment development. Pen-and-sepia-ink. Designer unknown.

3-15. The control of space in graphic terms. Perspective drawing of Queen of Heaven Cemetery garden crypt, New Baltimore, Pennsylvania. Pen-and-ink. Harley Ellington Pierce Yee and Associates, Inc.

Space may be easily understood intellectually; however, it is necessary to practice working with space to understand it graphically. One must make several hundred sketches, drawings, and paintings before learning to control graphic space, as well as any other hidden factors that make up a picture (figs. 3-15, 3-16, 3-17, C-12, and C-13).

Generating space through action is also an impressive dimension

of these drawings. Energy emanating from the pictures has been transposed in graphic terms through an understanding of the action visually observed when a form is in motion, as in figure 3-11. A figure sitting on a park bench appears almost flat, especially in the distance. However, a figure in motion has dynamic lines, reflecting new dimensional qualities of space around the figure. We realize that a figure at rest in nature must have arrived at this position through action. Usually the figure

3-16. Controlling graphic space, including such factors as tension, movement and shape impact, requires constant practice. Perspective drawing to the side of Queen of Heaven Cemetery garden crypt, New Baltimore, Pennsylvania. Pen-and-ink. Harley Ellington Pierce Yee and Associates, Inc.

in nature moves into various positions from some inert position that can be used as reference. This is comparable to observing extreme positions of a gate, open to closed; a coin at rest and spinning; or a plant form at rest and being blown in the wind. The positions through which the figure moves represent distinct intervals in a time sequence. Our choices are to see the figure in a frozen pose and draw it as if it were a statue or to see the pose as an occurrence at a given instant of an action in time.

Conceived as an occurrence in a time sequence, the figures in many of these drawings were derived by envisioning them as being in a particular position in space—through arcs representing phases of action. The figure volumes, implied action through discontinuous lines, reflect what they are doing—a manifestation of forces. Sutton used this method of depicting a form (human and nature) moving in time to create a dynamic picture and lend animation to his subjects.

C-12. Residence. Pen-and-sepia-ink. Designer unknown.

C-13. Residence. Pen-and-
sepia-ink. Designer unknown.

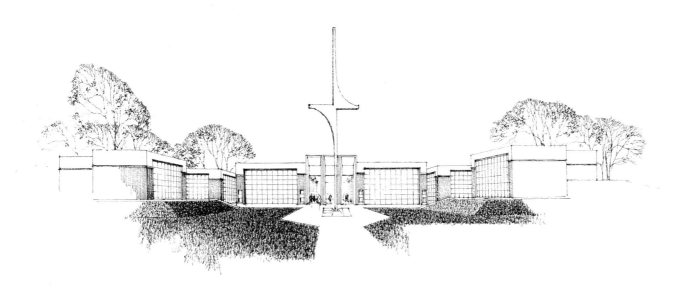

3-17. Everything revolves around a central focal point. Central perspective study, New Baltimore, Pennslyvania. Pen-and-ink. Harley Ellington Pierce Yee and Associates, Inc.

Balancing line and area to achieve space is another important attribute of graphic space, suggesting a relation of line to area (figs. C-14, C-15). Line creates a certain visual activity and simultaneously generates area. An area, which in drawing normally suggests only white paper, also creates visual impact—and therefore a balance between the two is desirable. In some drawings, the line often becomes overactive because of the artist's emphasis on aspects of the subject matter. Every object given similar importance also repeats line qualities and destroys graphic space—often indicative of the use of mechanical line qualities. For similar reasons, the unweighted line made with an unflexible point can become quite noticeable. Moreover, the so-

3-18. When line and area are in balance, a great sense of space is achieved. Perspective study of Oaks of Bloomfield Hills, Michigan, Site Condominiums. Pen-and-ink. Dave Sellards, Architect.

called light, faint, or sensitive line often becomes too delicate and hardly noticeable. Too much line activity (or weight) overemphasizes the line as a design factor, forcing us to view the line first and flattening out the picture. Conversely, too much insistence on area usually leads to a feeling of emptiness, remoteness, and often a sense of flatness—space is reduced to a minimum. When line and area are in balance, a great sense of space is felt throughout the form and structure of an illustration.

C-14. Residential complex. Pen-and-sepia-ink. Designer unknown.

C-15. Shopping complex. Pen-and-sepia-ink. Designer unknown.

3-19. An awareness of relative line thickness, pen speed, and movement are strong attributes of beautiful drawings. Oaks of Bloomfield Hills, Michigan, Site Condominiums. Pen-and-ink. Dave Sellards, Architect.

This line-area balance also plays an important role in the communication of scale in a composition. An awareness of relative line thicknesses and eventually pen speed and movement contributed strongly to Sutton's abilities to communicate beautifully in quick, concise sketch-notes to his clients, who were often architects in need of many views of design concepts, to show clients and to discuss in their offices (figs. 3-18, 3-19).

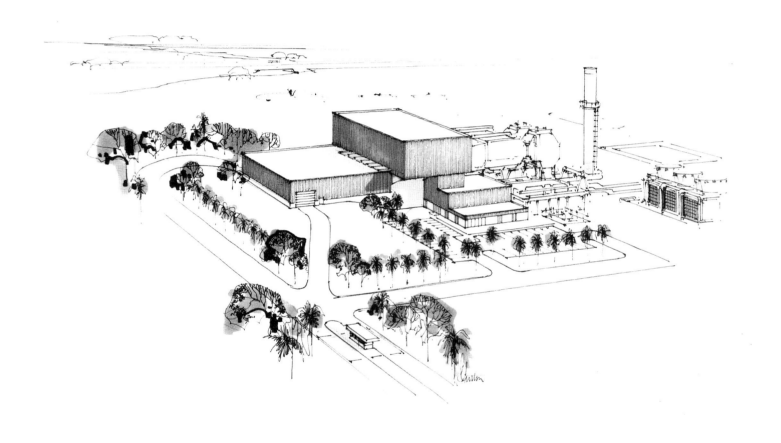

4-1. Proposal sketch for Energy Resource Recovery Plan, scheme A. Felt pen on paper (preliminary study). BEI Associates, Inc.

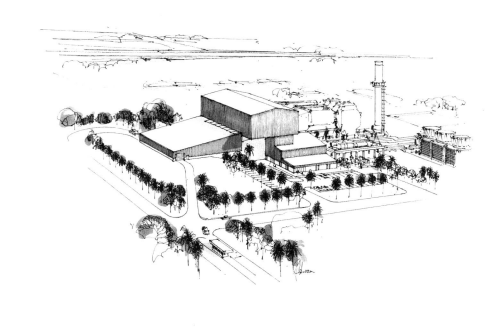

4-2. Proposal sketch for Energy Resource Recovery Plan, scheme B. Felt pen on paper (preliminary study). BEI Associates, Inc.

# Part Four: Refined Illustrations

Most drawings produced in an architectural office following another's instructions owe something to the artist's imagination. The illustrations in this part concentrate first on drawings that show the artist thinking on paper, his mind working in a preliminary graphic made before painting and rendering. The aim is to look at the role drawing has played in the creation of the finished illustrative work and to discuss the relationship between this role of drawing as process and the development of drawing in an artistic form (figs. 4-1, 4-2).

4-3. Graphic impression with focal point established at the eye level. Interior sketch study of United Technologies's Pratt & Whitney jet engine rebuild facility, Southington, Connecitcut. Felt pen on paper. Giffels Associates, Inc.

## Graphic Impressions

Although not all illustrators make drawings as rehearsals for final illustrations, many have found that a drawing helps to develop an idea in much the same way as words help to clarify thought. The activity of drawing converts an idea into lines and other marks on paper, exciting the mind and encouraging the transmittal of creative thinking (fig. 4-3).

Of course, everyone who draws does not follow this same procedure. Drawings have been used as a means of explaining what a completed work in other media (and often in three dimensions) will look like, and such drawings have often been made (as discussed in the introduction) to obtain a commission either privately, publicly, or through competition (figs. 4-4, 4-5).

4-4. Rendering made to obtain a commission. General Motors Hydromatic Dynamometer Test Cells, Ypsilanti, Michigan. Tempera on illustration board. BEI Associates, Inc.

4-5. Rendering made to obtain a commission. General Motors Hydromatic Dynamometer Test Cells, Ypsilanti, Michigan. Tempera on illustration board. BEI Associates, Inc.

4-6. Proposal drawing made in association with a rendered painting. Energy Resource Recovery Plan, Babylon, New York, view looking northeast. Pen-and-ink. BEI Associates, Inc.

The Italian word *modelli* is sometimes used to suggest drawings used as preliminary studies for a rendering (figs. 4-6, 4-7, and 4-8). Because these works are intended to impress a prospective client, they are often more finished than the sketches made by the artist for his own use during the creation of a work (figs. 4-9, 4-10). Helping the client to see what a proposed design will look like or to enable the designer to discuss alternatives is the objective of these more refined drawings and paintings (figs. 4-11, 4-12, 4-13, and 4-14).

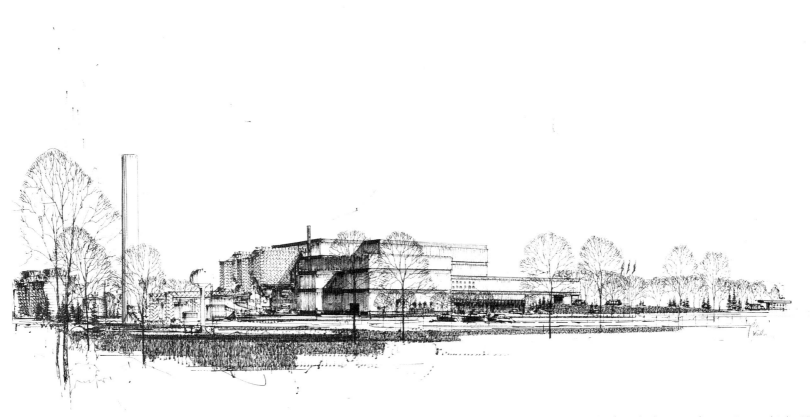

4-7. Proposal drawing made in association with a rendered painting. Energy Resource Recovery Plan, Babylon, New York, view looking southwest. Pen-and-ink. BEI Associates, Inc.

Although a design concept may suggest the use of certain tools and graphic media, the illustrator usually imagines the look of a future project when drawn with a particular tool or material. A particular work is given its form by the way in which the tools are used, combined with the artist's natural drawing abilities.

For some artists, such as Robert Sutton, the relationship between tool and usage is broad as opposed to narrow. Obviously, it is not the artist's mastery of technique alone that contributes to the quality of an illustration (figs. 4-15, 4-16).

4-8. Rendering of Energy Resource Recovery Plant, Babylon, New York. Tempera on illustration board. BEI Associates, Inc.

4-9. Proposal drawing made in association with a rendered painting. Resource Recovery Facility, Hennepin County, Minnesota. Felt pen and wash on illustration board. BEI Associates, Inc.

4-10. Proposal drawing made in association with a rendered painting. Resource Recovery Facility, Warren County, New Jersey. Felt pen and wash on illustration board. BEI Associates, Inc.

4-11. Rendering of industrial energy facility. Tempera on illustration board. BEI Associates, Inc.

4-12. Rendering of industrial energy facility. Tempera on illustration board. BEI Associates, Inc.

4-13. Rendering of industrial resource recovery facility. Tempera on illustration board. BEI Associates, Inc.

4-14. Rendering of industrial resource recovery facility. Tempera on illustration board. BEI Associates, Inc.

4-15. Rendering of residential design. Pen-and-ink. Designer unknown.

The interaction between the tool and its application, *technique* in the best sense of the term, works in service of the illustrative concept and is neither detached nor separate from the central idea behind the work. In the worst sense, *technique* is a separate and often unrelated aspect of the work and appears as surface treatment without inherent qualities of design related to the central idea of the illustration. The tools and materials of the drawing must therefore be integral to and viewed in collaboration with the artist's vision, giving life to the subject's forms and not becoming the subject itself (figs. 4-17, 4-18).

4-16. Rendering of residential design. Pen-and-ink. Designer unknown.

C-16. High-rise office building. Pen-and-ink with watercolor wash. Designer unknown.

C-17. Office tower. Pen-and-ink with wash. Designer unknown.

4-17. The tools and materials of drawing complement the subject; they do not themselves become the subject. Sketch study of interior scheme for Oakland University Library, Rochester, Michigan. Felt pen on paper. BEI Associates, Inc.

The surface qualities in Sutton's illustrations in figures 4-19 and 4-20 stem from the marks of the pen and brush, which appear to be carefully sculpted to define a relationship between natural and man-made structures. The texture breaks down the light into small parts and produces a visual reference of value gradations against the architecture. Here tool and application serve to heighten the dialog between background and central subject matter. The careful placement of line and texture at the sides and middle serve to define the foreground and distinguish major elements.

4-18. The technique of drawing supports the simplicity of graphic execution. Rendering of high-rise office building lobby. Mixed media. BEI Associates, Inc.

C-18. Office tower. Pen-and-ink with wash. Designer unknown.

C-19. Office tower. Pen-and-ink with wash. Designer unknown.

4-19. In the light, texture breaks into small parts and produces value gradations. Study drawing of suburban office complex. Felt pen on paper. Designer unknown.

Sutton's sensuous yet functional tool marks are not separate from the action of the form. The active strokes in areas of entourage force the eye upward, aided by the plan of many vignetted compositions. His broken contours seem to melt the major sections, organize space, and direct the focus, rather than calling attention to their own virtuosity. As in all of his work, the handling of tools, be they ink, marker, or paint, is intentional, a search for a clear staging of the subject matter and supporting imagery.

4-20. Rendering of University of Michigan Hospital parking structure, Ann Arbor, Michigan. Tempera on illustration board. Harley Ellington Pierce Yee and Associates, Inc.

## Urban Renderings and Industrial Projects

The drawings and paintings included in this section are examples of refined urban illustrations that were created well before the design was built, usually in an effort to win a design commission or contract (figs. C-16, C-17, C-18, C-19, C-20, C-21, C-22, and C-23). The clarity of their form and description stems from the illustrator's skill in visualizing what the intended

C-20. Office building complex. Pen-and-ink with wash. Designer unknown.

C-21. Library and complex Pen-and-ink with wash. Designer unknown.

4-21. Rendering of high-rise office building swimming pool and health club, Detroit, Michigan. Mixed media. BEI Associates, Inc.

design concept will look like, often along with its landscaping, building material, and/or interior design scheme. These works can be appreciated for their aesthetic qualities alone, without thought to the original reason for their existence, which is nevertheless an important factor contributing to their appearance (figs. 4-21, 4-22, 4-23, 4-24, 4-25, 4-26, 4-27, 4-28, 4-29, and 4-30).

4-22. Rendering of high-rise office building conference room, Detroit, Michigan. Mixed media. BEI Associates, Inc.

C-22. Office building complex. Pen-and-ink with wash. Designer unknown.

C-23. Office entrance. Pen-and-ink with wash. Designer unknown.

4-23. Rendering of high-rise office building outside entrance, Detroit, Michigan. Mixed media. BEI Associates, Inc.

4-24. Rendering of high-rise office building, Detroit, Michigan.
Mixed media. BEI Associates, Inc.

4-25. Rendering of General Dynamics Land Systems Group lobby. Felt pen on illustration board. Giffels Associates, Inc.

4-26. Rendering of General Dynamics Land Systems Group cafeteria. Felt pen on illustration board. Giffels Associates, Inc.

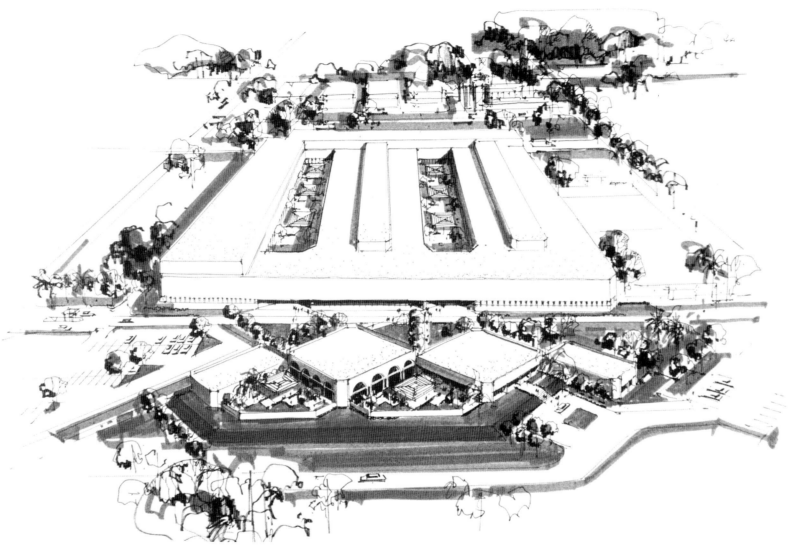

4-27. Study drawing of industrial plant in Middle East. Felt pen on paper. Giffels Associates, Inc.

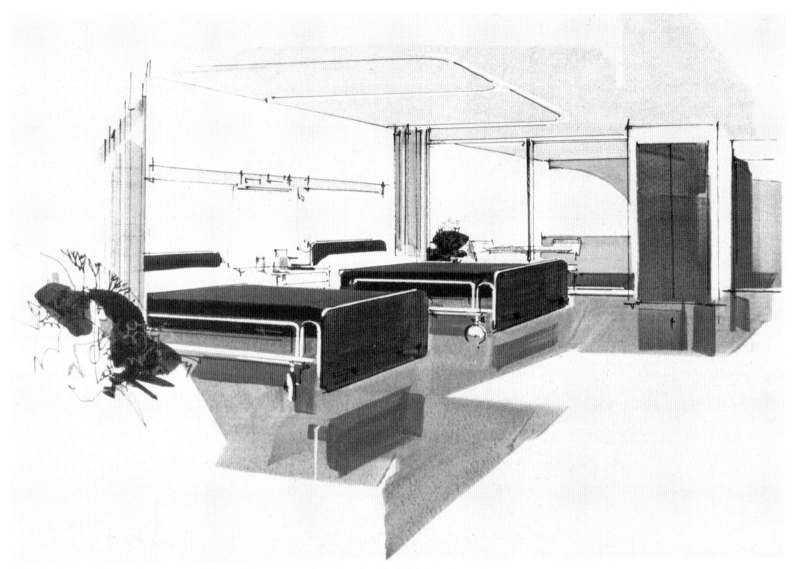

4-28. Rendering of hospital room in Middle East. Tempera on illustration board. Giffels Associates, Inc.

4-29. Rendering of suburban office complex. Tempera on illustration board. Designer unknown.

4-30. Rendering of General Motors Hydromatic Dynamometer Test Cells, Ypsilanti, Michigan. Tempera on illustration board. BEI Associates, Inc.

5-1. Flower arrangement. Acrylic on canvas. Collection of the artist's family.

5-2. Study of wildflowers. Watercolor. Collection of the artist's family.

# Part Five:
# Painter's Response

This final part reinforces some of the ideas developed throughout the book, using artistic drawings and paintings by Robert Sutton as illustrations, and explores still further the possibilities that exist in the art of drawing and painting.

This book has emphasized throughout the need to practice and rephrase when drawing natural and man-made forms, until one can create them almost from memory, until they become as automatic as handwriting. In this context it is appropriate to reproduce a few of Sutton's color paintings in black-and-white to demonstrate his graphic response to and phrasing of nature and

5-3. Landscape. Watercolor. Collection of the artist's family.

5-4. Barn scene. Acrylic on canvas. Collection of the artist's family.

those related forms that he loved and selected as subjects for his art.

## Nature

Some of Sutton's landscape painting consists of invented and remembered forms from nature. Discreetly hidden within the compositions are abstracted parts from a vast panorama of natural forms—abstract to representational—which he used so often in his architectural drawing and painting. These landscapes can be viewed as a stage for invention, experimentation with media, and graphic improvisation that can be found in part in his architectural subjects as well. Sutton normally places the viewer in the center of his subject matter and positions the subject directly in front of the viewer (figs. 5-1, 5-2, 5-3, 5-4, C-24, and C-25).

5-5. Horse and carriage. Watercolor. Collection of the artist's family.

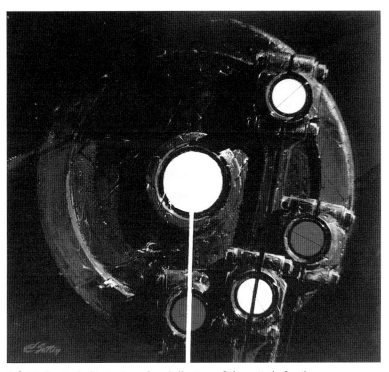

5-6. Mechanical object. Gouache. Collection of the artist's family.

## Objects and Human Form

More, perhaps than any other visual medium, drawing is a magical experience. In no other artform can one go so directly from thought to image, unencumbered by materials or laborious planning. With experience, Sutton was able to refine his thoughts in a direct manner and without complicated techniques. As an immediate form of creative expression, drawing accommodated many of his methods and attitudes, whether he was reacting to his environment, working from memory, improvising, or constructing complex architectural relationships. Whether the subject was natural or architectural, whether his intent was improvisation or specific representation, much of his work has a built-in economy of conception and performance. An economy of means in drawing is somewhat deceptive to the novice, who is unfamiliar with methods of reducing a subject to its graphic essence as well as with choosing tools for communication. The accumulation of experience and personality, however, leads to a vision capable of transmitting lucid forms and concepts in most unusual ways (figs. 5-5, 5-6, 5-7, 5-8, C-26, and C-27).

5-7. Painting of Ann Sutton Wiedlea. Acrylic on canvas. Collection of the artist's family.

5-8. Study of Ann at play. Acrylic on canvas. Collection of the artist's family.

5-9. Rendering of The World Trade Center proposal, Bangkok, Thailand. Tempera and Conté crayon on illustration board. Yamaski and Associates. Drawings Collection of the College of Architecture and Design, Lawrence Technological University.

5-10. Brochure cover illustration. Mixed media. Superior Corporation.

## Architecture

Many artists and illustrators admire the drawing facility and improvisational skill demonstrated by Sutton that they do not inherently possess. His emphasis was placed on the implementation of methods versus simple duplication. Many of his paintings clearly demonstrate improvisation with materials and shapes, a kind of "thinking within" the work coupled with a developed ability to select the most important attributes to depict. His lifetime of experience led to the development of an enlightened

C-24. Flower arrangement. Acrylic on canvas. Collection of the artist's family.

C-25. Landscape. Watercolor. Collection of the artist's family.

5-11. Memorial study. Acrylic on canvas. Collection of the artist's family.

5-12. Memorial study, Acrylic on canvas. Collection of the artist's family.

attitude that inspired many around him to see their environment in a different and possibly new way (figs. 5-9, 5-10, 5-11, 5-12, 5-13, 5-14, 5-15, 5-16, C-28, and C-29).

These images reveal an artist's vision and skill in the creation of something new—a *formative experience* in life and art. This process called invention or improvisation begins when the illustrator, provoked by an image or thought, puts pen to paper.

C-26. Horse and carriage. Watercolor. Collection of the artist's family.

C-27. Painting of Ann Sutton Wiedlea. Acrylic on canvas. Collection of the artist's family.

5-13. Barn scene. Watercolor. Collection of the artist's family.

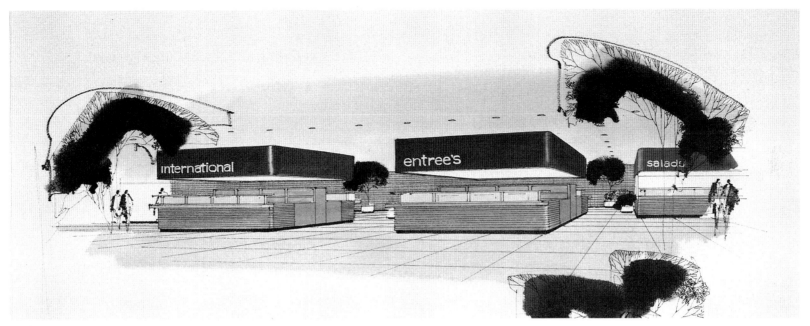

5-14. Proposal for food corporation. Mixed media. Designer unknown.

C-28. High-rise apartment complex. Tempera on illustration board. Designer unknown.

INTERNATIONAL TERMINAL
DETROIT METROPOLITAN WAYNE COUNTY AIRPORT
LOUIS G. REDSTONE ASSOCIATES INC.

C-29. International Terminal Building, Metropolitan Airport, Detroit, Michigan. Tempera on illustration board. Collection of City of Detroit.

5-15. Rendering for industrial facility. Tempera on illustration board. Designer unknown.

5-16. Rendering of hotel complex. Tempera on illustration board. Designer unknown.

# Bibliography

Atkin, William Wilson. *Architectural Presentation Techniques*. New York: Van Nostrand Reinhold, 1976.

Betti, Claudia, and Teel Sale. *Drawing: A Contemporary Approach*. New York: Holt, Rinehart and Winston, 1980.

Bishop, Minor L. *Architectural Renderings by Winners of the Birch Burdette Long Memorial Prize*. New York: The Architectural League of New York, 1965.

Bro, Lu. *Drawing: A Studio Guide*. New York: W. W. Norton and Company, 1978.

Chaet, Bernard. *The Art of Drawing*. New York: Holt, Rinehart and Winston, 1978.

Goldstein, Nathan. *The Art of Responsive Drawing*. Englewood Cliffs, New Jersey: Prentice-Hall, 1973.

Graham, Donald W. *Composing Pictures*. New York: Van Nostrand Reinhold, 1970.

Jacoby, Helmut. *The New Techniques of Architectural Rendering*. New York: Reinhold Publishing Corporation, 1961.

Kautzky, Theodore. *Pencil Pictures*. New York: Reinhold Publishing Corporation, 1947.

——. *Ways with Watercolor*. New York: Reinhold Publishing Corporation, 1963.

Lever, Jill, and Margaret Richardson. *The Architect as Artist*. New York: Rizzoli International Publications, 1984.

Linton, Harold, and Roy J. Strickfaden. *Architectural Sketching in Markers*. New York: Van Nostrand Reinhold, 1991.

Loomis, Andrew. *Creative Illustration*. New York: Viking, 1957.

Myerscough-Walker, Raymond. *The Perspectivist*. London: Pitman, 1958.

Oles, Paul Stevenson. *Architectural Illustration: The Value Delineation Process*. New York: Van Nostrand Reinhold, 1979.

——. *Drawing the Future: A Decade of Architecture in Perspective Drawings*. New York: Van Nostrand Reinhold, 1988.

Oliver, Robert S. *The Complete Sketch*. New York: Van Nostrand Reinhold, 1989.

Pennt, Wolfgang. *Expressionist Architecture in Drawings*. New York: Van Nostrand Reinhold, 1985.

Porter, Tom. *Architectural Drawing*. New York: Van Nostrand Reinhold, 1990.

Rochon, Richard, and Harold Linton. *Color in Architectural Illustration*. New York: Van Nostrand Reinhold, 1989.

Stamp, Gavin. *The Great Perspectivists*. New York: Rizzoli International Publications, 1982.

Watson, Ernest W. *The Art of Pencil Drawing*. New York: Watson-Guptill Publications, 1968.

# Index

Index